CLASSIC RIDES

CLASSIC GTOs

BY CLAIRE ROMAINE

INVESTIGATE!

Enslow PUBLISHING

Please visit our website, www.enslow.com. For a free color catalog of all our high-quality books, call toll free 1-800-398-2504 or fax 1-877-980-4454.

Library of Congress Cataloging-in-Publication Data

Names: Romaine, Claire, author.
Title: Classic GTOs / Claire Romaine.
Description: New York : Enslow Publishing, [2021] | Series: Classic rides | Includes index.
Identifiers: LCCN 2019047821 | ISBN 9781978518056 (library binding) | ISBN 9781978518032 (paperback) | ISBN 9781978518049 (6 Pack) | ISBN 9781978518063 (ebook)
Subjects: LCSH: Sports cars—Juvenile literature.
Classification: LCC TL236 .R66 2021 | DDC 629.222—dc23
LC record available at https://lccn.loc.gov/2019047821

Published in 2021 by
Enslow Publishing
101 West 23rd Street, Suite #240
New York, NY 10011

Designer: Katelyn E. Reynolds
Editor: Therese Shea

Photo credits: Cover, pp. 1 (left GTO), 22 Kevin M. McCarthy/Shutterstock.com; cover, p. 1 (middle GTO) Car Culture ® Collection/Getty Images Plus; cover, p. 1 (right GTO) © iStockphoto.com/WendellandCarolyn; cover, pp. 1–32 (series chrome font) Mott Jordan/Shutterstock.com; cover, pp. 1–32 (series background) Sylvie Bouchard/Shutterstock.com; pp. 5 (Ferrari), 8, 9 Pit Stock/Shutterstock.com; pp. 5 (Mitsubishi), 14 Thaian07/ Wikipedia.org; pp. 5 (Audi), 17 Brian Snelson (https://www.flickr.com/photos/32659528@N00)/Wikipedia.org; pp. 5 (Pontiac), 21 Greg Gjerdingen (https://www.flickr.com/people/52900873@N07) from Willmar, USA/Wikipedia.org; pp. 5 (Noble), 28 johnbraid/Shutterstock.com; p. 6 Sfoskett~commonswiki/Wikipedia.org; p. 7 (main) Don Heiny/Corbis Documentary/Getty Images Plus; p. 7 (inset) GP Library/Universal Images Group via Getty Images; p. 10 (both) National Motor Museum/Heritage Images/Getty Images; p. 11 Thesupermat/Wikipedia.org; p. 13 Mytho88/Wikipedia.org; p. 15 Cloudrunner at English Wikipedia/Wikipedia.org; p. 16 Timmäää/Wikipedia.org; p. 18 Bob Harmeyer/Archive Photos/Getty Images; p. 19 CJM Photography/Alamy Stock Photo; p. 20 Bob D'Olivo/The Enthusiast Network via Getty Images/Getty Images; p. 23 Tony Savino/Shutterstock.com; p. 24 tratong/Shutterstock.com; p. 25 Michael Barera/Wikipedia.org; p. 27 Dmitry Zaltsman/Shutterstock.com.

Portions of this work were originally authored by Heather Moore Niver and published as *GTOs*. All new material this edition authored by Claire Romaine.

Printed in the United States of America

Contents

WORDS IN THE GLOSSARY APPEAR IN **BOLD** TYPE THE FIRST TIME THEY ARE USED IN THE TEXT.

THE ABCS OF GTOs

The letters GTO stand for *Gran Turismo Omologato*. That's Italian for "Grand Touring Homologated." This label once meant that a vehicle was qualified to race in certain competitions. Though many car fans have forgotten the actual meaning of the letters over the years, they haven't forgotten the **classic** cars with the GTO label. To them, GTO means fast and stylish!

Just as many makes of vehicles have been on the racetrack over the years, many companies have made GTOs. One of the most celebrated was created by the Italian carmaker Ferrari.

GET THE FACTS!

When Ferrari made its first GTO in the early 1960s, it could only get the GTO qualification if it produced 100 high-performance cars for street driving. This meant regular people could drive cars similar to the racetrack vehicles!

WHO PRODUCED GTOS?

FERRARI

MITSUBISHI

AUDI

GTO CARMAKERS

PONTIAC

NOBLE

FERRARI GTOs

FERRARI 250 GTO ENGINE

Some say Ferrari only made road cars like its 250 GTO so it could make cars for the racetrack. The Ferrari 250 GTO was created to be **aerodynamic**, not good-looking. However, it turned out to be both. It was tested on a racetrack and even in a **wind tunnel**. Only the most important features were included to keep its weight low.

GET THE FACTS!

Ferrari built only 39 GTOs, not the 100 the race rules required. The company argued its 250 GTO was like its 250 GT. The race committee agreed. The Ferrari 250 GTO won the International Championship for GT Manufacturers in 1962, 1963, and 1964.

Motor Trend Classic magazine called the 250 GTO the greatest Ferrari of all time. Some car fans go further. They claim it's the greatest sports car *ever*!

*IN 2018, A 1962 FERRARI 250 GTO WAS SOLD AT AN **AUCTION** FOR MORE THAN $48 MILLION! IT'S THE MOST EXPENSIVE CAR EVER SOLD AT AN AUCTION.*

GET THE FACTS!

The 288 was named for its 2.8-liter engine with eight **cylinders**, also called a V-8. The car may not have raced, but Ferrari couldn't make enough 288 GTOs to satisfy eager car fans! The company increased production to meet demands.

Twenty years after the 250 GTO, Ferrari came out with the 288 GTO. The biggest advancement from other Ferrari road cars was its stronger, lighter body. In fact, it was 700 pounds (318 kg) lighter than similar models!

Ferrari made this GTO to race, just like the 250 GTO. The 288 GTO reached 60 miles (97 km) per hour in just 4.5 seconds. Its top speed was 189 miles (304 km) per hour. Unfortunately, the race to show off the car was canceled because of racetrack safety issues.

THE FERRARI GTOS BUILT IN 1984 AND 1985 ARE EVERY CAR COLLECTOR'S DREAM! JUST 272 WERE MADE.

In 2011, Ferrari introduced its 599 GTO. Ferrari called the car its "most extreme sports car." With a powerful engine, the vehicle could zoom from 0 to 60 miles (97 km) per hour in just 3.1 seconds. In tests, it reached a top speed of 208 miles (335 km) per hour! A car that fast has to stop quickly, so the 599 had light, high-performance brakes.

599 GTO ENGINE

THE PRICE OF A 599 GTO BEGAN AT $450,000!

The 599 GTO was based on the racetrack model—the 599XX. As Ferrari did with its other GTOs, it made only a limited number: 599.

GET THE FACTS!

Normally, the weight of a car is the only thing that forces its tires down at high speeds. Fast turns can be dangerous. The Ferrari's rear spoiler uses wind to generate force that keeps the car from lifting and tipping over.

MITSUBISHI GTOs

Mitsubishi's entry into the GTO market was its 1970 Colt Galant GTO. It had an eye-catching body. The Japanese carmaker described its shape as "dynawedge." It sported a long hood and a ducktail rear, similar to the shape of a duck's upturned tail. Galant models for years to come used a similar design, or shape.

GET THE FACTS!

The original Mitsubishi GTO was designed by Hiroaki Kamisago. The company sent him to study at the Art Center College of Design in Pasadena, California. The car's style honored American ***muscle cars****, such as the Ford Mustang and Pontiac Firebird.*

MITSUBISHI HAD PLANS TO ENTER THE MOTORSPORTS WORLD WITH ITS GTOS, BUT THAT NEVER HAPPENED. THE GALANT GTO WOULD LAST ONLY UNTIL 1975.

The 1975 Galant GTO featured Mitsubishi's Silent Shaft **technology**. This made the engine run smoothly and quietly. Other automobile companies liked this technology so much that they paid Mitsubishi to use it.

MOTOR TREND MAGAZINE NAMED THE MITSUBISHI MODEL CALLED THE 3000GT VR-4 ITS **IMPORT** CAR OF THE YEAR FOR 1991.

The next time Mitsubishi produced a GTO was 1990. The car was a stylish sports coupe, or two-door car. It was called the 3000GT in most places. Its "active" rear wing lengthened at high speeds to reduce lifting force. **All-wheel drive** and tough brakes made drivers confident on the road.

GET THE FACTS!

Mitsubishi's GTO was known as the Mitsubishi 3000GT in every country except Japan. Mitsubishi was concerned that car experts wouldn't like the GTO name on a Japanese car. The cars were built at Mitsubishi's plant in Nagoya, Japan.

Unfortunately, these features made the Mitsubishi GTO heavier than other sports coupes. In addition, some complained that it wasn't large enough to allow tall people to sit up straight! The last of these fast, good-looking cars was made in 1999.

ACTIVE REAR WING

AUDI GTOs

In the late 1980s, the carmaker Audi came out with a GTO that became famous on the racing circuit. The Audi 90 Quattro IMSA GTO competed in the IMSA (International Motor Sports Association) racing series in North America.

GET THE FACTS!

The Audi GTO race car didn't look much like a street Audi. The engine's exhaust pipe, the pipe where the gases escape, came out the passenger door! The car had a special front air dam and rear wing to combat lift on the track.

This car's amazing engine produced 720 **horsepower**, enough to compete with any American race car. It was also all-wheel drive, which made a big difference on the track. The Audi GTO dominated the 1989 IMSA season. However, IMSA then banned all-wheel drive cars, so the Audi GTO could no longer compete.

THE SHOW *TOP GEAR* NAMED THE 1989 AUDI 90 QUATTRO IMSA GTO ONE OF ITS 50 COOLEST RACE CARS.

GET THE FACTS!

One of the original S4 GTOs was reassembled for a few European racing series, such as the German STT. It was retired in 1998. A replica, or copy, of the Audi S4 GTO can be seen at the Audi/VW Museum in South Africa.

The Audi GTO reappeared in South Africa in 1992. The Wesbank racing series required that competing cars had to be sold in South Africa. To fulfill this requirement, the 90 Quattro IMSA GTO was converted into the Audi S4 GTO.

AUDI 90 QUATTRO IMSA GTO

FAMOUS RACE CARS, SUCH AS THE AUDI S4 GTO HERE, CAN SOMETIMES BE SEEN IN SPECIAL EVENTS, SUCH AS THE GOODWOOD FESTIVAL OF SPEED.

The S4 easily won its first race. In 1993, a second S4 GTO joined the team. Together, the two conquered the Wesbank series. By 1995, this series required that cars have V-8 engines. The Audis had five-cylinder engines. This was the end of Audi GTOs in major racing events.

PONTIAC GTOs

JOHN DELOREAN

The year 1964 is often said to be the beginning of the muscle-car age. That year, John DeLorean of General Motors' Pontiac division issued the Pontiac GTO. While it wasn't made to race like the Ferrari GTO, the Pontiac GTO had speed and power. The mightiest V-8 engine offered boasted 348 horsepower.

GET THE FACTS!

John DeLorean is known as the father of the GTO. He put the V-8 engine in the Pontiac LeMans to create the GTO. DeLorean was praised for keeping the company on the cutting edge. After leaving Pontiac, he started his own company.

The Pontiac GTO also had hood scoops, which are raised parts that increase airflow to the engine to boost power. However, the GTO hood scoops were fake! They were added to make the car look tougher.

THE 1964 PONTIAC GTO WAS ALSO OFFERED AS A CONVERTIBLE, OR A CAR WITH A ROOF THAT CAN BE LOWERED OR REMOVED.

GET THE FACTS!

Every year, Pontiac updated its GTO. Buyers kept an eye on changes. For example, the 1968 GTO had an Endura rubber bumper. It made the car look like it didn't have a bumper. TV ads showed John DeLorean pounding it with a hammer!

Beginning with the 1968 model year, the Pontiac GTO got a curvier look. Length and height were reduced. The headlights were side by side rather than stacked—or they were hidden! It was *Motor Trend*'s Car of the Year.

THE JUDGE WAS AN OPTION PACKAGE FOR THE REGULAR GTO MODEL. AN OPTION PACKAGE IS A LIST OF FEATURES ADDED TO A CAR MODEL.

A special 1969 Pontiac GTO was named "the Judge" after a line from a funny TV show: "Here comes da judge!" It had a black **grille**, stripes, and stickers that said "The Judge." People didn't need to be told when this Judge was coming!

BUYERS COULD CHOOSE A COLOR CALLED ORBIT ORANGE FOR THEIR 1970 GTO JUDGE. IT ACTUALLY LOOKED YELLOW!

The 1970 GTO Judge was given a fresh front end, including newly designed headlights. But the Judge's rule was almost over. The government passed laws that required cars to release less pollution and be more **fuel-efficient**. In response, later GTO engines produced less horsepower. They became muscle cars without muscle.

GET THE FACTS!

In the 1960s, the GTO inspired songs such as "GTO" by Ronnie and the Daytonas. In "Mighty GTO," the musical act Jan and Dean sang, "Hold your clutch down tight, rev it up to go / You're about to do business with my mighty GTO."

In 1973 and 1974, the GTO was just an option package on other models. The Endura bumper was replaced with steel. Inside the car, everything became basic and plain. The 1974 model was the last of the Pontiac GTOs for many years.

1970 GTO ENGINE

In 1999, a Pontiac GTO concept car got people excited about its reappearance. A concept car shows possible designs and features but isn't sold to the public. Finally, in 2004, Pontiac released a GTO model—the Holden Monaro—which came from Australia. It was the first GTO without a fake hood scoop but was the fastest yet.

The 2005 and 2006 GTOs were even speedier. The hood scoops came back, as did GTO horsepower. These GTOs could drive 1/4 mile (400 m) in 13.5 seconds! Sadly, these were the last Pontiac GTOs.

GET THE FACTS!

Monaro production ended in Australia, so 2006 was the last year for the Pontiac GTO. General Motors ended the entire Pontiac brand in 2009. The United States had entered a hard economic period, and fewer people were buying cars.

PONTIAC GTO FANS OFTEN CALL THIS CAR "THE GOAT."
NO ONE IS SURE WHERE THIS NICKNAME COMES FROM!
2005 PONTIAC GTO
0–60 MILES (0–97 KM) PER HOUR IN 4.7 SECONDS

NOBLE GTOs

Want to build your own GTO? Car designer and race car driver Lee Noble made that possible in 2000 with his Noble M12 GTO. It's a "kit car," or "component car." It arrives in two boxes. Once put together, it can reach 60 miles (97 km) per hour in a blazing 3.3 seconds. It's rare to see this GTO, though.

No matter who makes it, GTO remains a name for a speedy car with style. Car fans love the classic GTOs of the past and look forward to more in the future.

GET THE FACTS!

Motorcycle fans know GTOs aren't just cars. Bridgestone made the 1967 350 GTO motorcycle. Some say this stylish bike was the best motorcycle of its time. It's called a "scrambler," meaning it could be driven on or off the road.

A TIMELINE OF GTO MODELS

- 1962 — FIRST MODEL YEAR FOR FERRARI'S 250 GTO
- 1964 — PONTIAC'S FIRST GTO
- 1970 — MITSUBISHI'S FIRST COLT GALANT GTO
- 1974 — LAST MODEL YEAR FOR PONTIAC GTOS FOR A TIME
- 1989 — AUDI 90 QUATTRO IMSA GTO IS CREATED FOR THE RACETRACK
- 1999 — MITSUBISHI'S LAST MODEL OF GTO
- 2000 — NOBLE M12 GTO CAR KIT IS RELEASED
- 2004 — PONTIAC'S HOLDEN MONARO GTO DEBUTS
- 2006 — LAST MODEL YEAR FOR THE PONTIAC GTO
- 2011 — FERRARI'S LAST GTO, THE 599 GTO, IS RELEASED

Glossary

aerodynamic Having a shape that improves airflow around a car to increase its speed.

all-wheel drive A system of moving a car that powers all four wheels instead of just the front or back wheels.

auction A sale of goods or property at which buyers bid against one another for items.

classic Describing something that is considered one of the best of its kind or something that has become popular over time.

cylinder A tube-shaped space in an engine in which a piston is pushed by the pressure or force of a fluid.

fuel-efficient The quality of being able to operate using little fuel, or without waste.

grille A metal screen on the front of a car that allows cool air into the engine.

horsepower A unit used to measure the power of an engine.

import A product brought into a country to be sold there.

muscle car A midsize sports car with a powerful engine built for speed.

technology A machine, piece of equipment, or process that is created by the latest scientific tools and methods.

wind tunnel A tunnel in which a current of air is blown around a car to determine its aerodynamic qualities.

FOR MORE INFORMATION

BOOKS

Caswell, Deanna. *Muscle Cars*. Mankato, MN: Black Rabbit Books, 2018.

West, David. *Race Cars*. Mankato, MN: Smart Apple Media, 2016.

WEBSITES

Ferrari 250 GTO: Everything You Need to Know
www.topgear.com/car-news/classic/ferrari-250-gto-everything-you-need-know
Check out facts about this amazing car.

GTO Association of America
www.gtoaa.org
Find information about where to see GTOs and more on this official site.

How Cars Work
auto.howstuffworks.com/car.htm
Learn more about cars and their engineering.

Index